Keyboards

Wendy Lynch

Heinemann LIBRARY

www.heinemann.co.uk/library
Visit our website to find out more information about **Heinemann Library** books.

To order:
☎ Phone ++44 (0)1865 888066
📄 Send a fax to ++44 (0)1865 314091
💻 Visit the Heinemann Bookshop at www.heinemann.co.uk/library to browse our catalogue and order online.

First published in Great Britain by Heinemann Library, Halley Court, Jordan Hill, Oxford
OX2 8EJ, a division of Reed Educational and Professional Publishing Ltd. Heinemann
is a registered trademark of Reed Educational & Professional Publishing Ltd.

OXFORD MELBOURNE AUCKLAND JOHANNESBURG BLANTYRE
GABORONE IBADAN PORTSMOUTH NH (USA) CHICAGO

Designed by Visual Image
Illustrations by Jane Watkins
Originated by Dot Gradations
Printed and bound in South China

ISBN 0 431 12904 5

05 04 03 02 01
10 9 8 7 6 5 4 3 2 1

British Library Cataloguing in Publication Data

Lynch, Wendy
Keyboards. – (Musical instruments)
1. Keyboard instruments – Juvenile literature
I. Title
786

Acknowledgements
The publishers would like to thank the following for permission to reproduce photographs: Ace Photo Agency p11,
Corbis pp20, 23, Gareth Boden pp9, 28, 29, Lebrecht collection pp17 (David Farrell), 26 (Kate Mount), Photodisc pp6,
7, 8, 18, 19, Powerstock (Zefa) p4, Redferns pp5 (Patrick Ford), 14, 25 (Ebet Roberts), 27 (Patrick Ford), Robert
Harding pp10, 21, Stone pp16 (Ian Shaw), 22, Superstock p24, Trevor Clifford p15.

Cover photograph reproduced with permission of Photodisc.

Every effort has been made to contact copyright holders of any material reproduced in this book.
Any omissions will be rectified in subsequent printings if notice is given to the Publisher.

Any words appearing in the text in bold, **like this**, are explained in the Glossary.

Contents

Making music together

There are many musical instruments in the world. Each instrument makes a different sound. We can make music together by playing these instruments in a band or an **orchestra**.

Bands and orchestras are made up of different groups of instruments. One of these groups is called keyboard instruments. You may find them in smaller bands like this **jazz** band.

What are keyboard instruments?

The piano, the organ, the harpsichord and the **synthesizer** are all keyboard instruments. They are called keyboard instruments because they are all played using a keyboard.

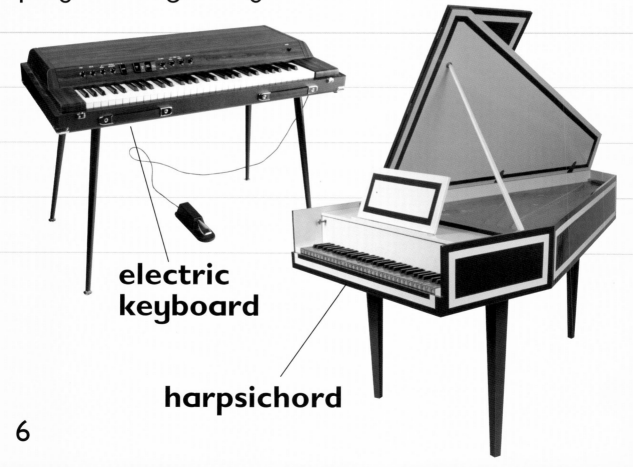

electric keyboard

harpsichord

A keyboard has many keys. You press the key to make a sound. Each key makes a different sound. This sound is a musical note.

grand piano

organ

vibraphone

The piano

The piano is a popular keyboard instrument. Children often learn to play the piano in school with a teacher.

You can play the piano with another person. This is called playing a piano duet. One player plays the keys on the left of the keyboard. The other plays the keys on the right.

Making a noise

The piano has black keys and white keys. These keys are in a pattern. The keys on the left of the keyboard play lower notes. The keys on the right play higher notes.

Inside the piano there is a string for each key. When you press a key a hammer hits the string. The strings that play the lower notes are wider than the strings for the higher notes.

How the sound is made

When a hammer hits a string inside the piano, this makes the string move quickly from side to side. This movement is called **vibration**.

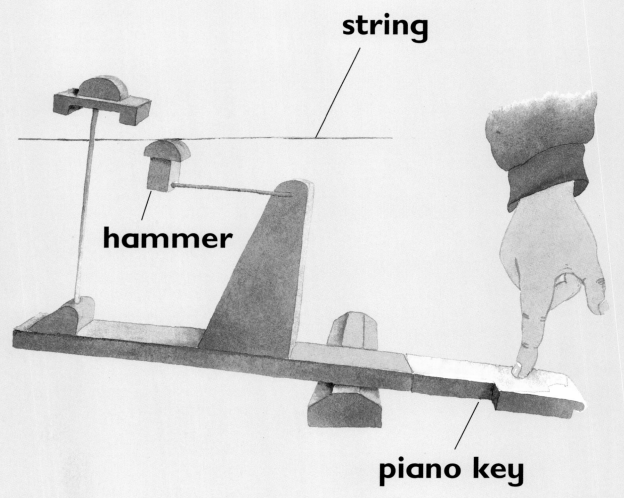

string

hammer

piano key

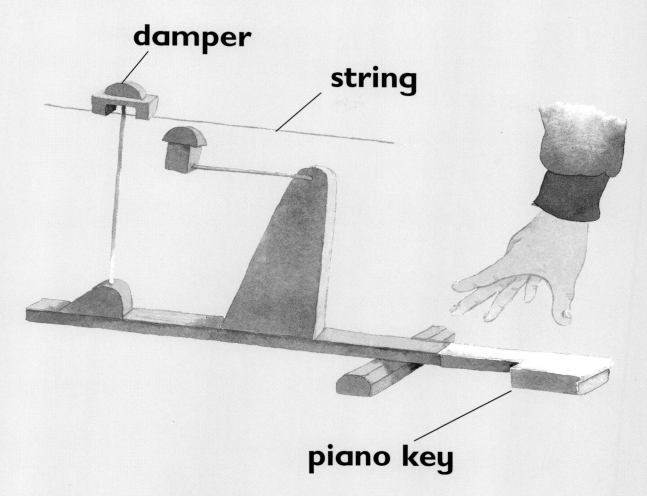

damper

string

piano key

The movement of the strings makes the air inside the piano vibrate. When air vibrates, it makes a sound. When you lift your finger from the piano keys, a piece of wood called a damper stops the string vibrating.

Types of piano

The **upright piano** is a popular piano. It takes less space than some other pianos. You can find upright pianos in schools, in houses and in public places like cafés and restaurants.

You can hear the grand piano in concerts. You can keep the lid of the grand piano open as you play. This means that the sound is stronger and richer.

Piano concert

In school, your teacher may play the piano to **accompany** singing or dancing or movement. Your teacher may play the piano for a **musical** you perform.

You may hear the piano on its own or with other musical instruments. In a piano **trio**, you can hear the piano, the violin and the cello.

Types of keyboard

The harpsichord has strings inside it, like the piano. When you press a key, a small piece of wood inside the harpsichord **plucks** the string.

The electric piano sounds very like an **upright piano**. It does not make music using strings and hammers. The sound is made by an electronic **amplifier**.

Organs and harmoniums

The organ has a keyboard but it is also a wind instrument. There is a link between each key and a pipe. When you press the key, air goes into a pipe. Each pipe makes a different sound.

The harmonium is a kind of organ. It has some **bellows** which hold the air. When you press the pedal you pump air into a **reed**. The reed **vibrates** and makes a sound.

The wider family

To play the accordion you press the keyboard and buttons. At the same time, you push and pull the **bellows** to make air move inside the accordion. This makes the sound.

The vibraphone has metal bars that look like a keyboard. You strike the bars using two hammers. You can hear the vibraphone in **jazz**.

Famous musicians and composers

A famous **composer** called Mozart started to learn the harpsichord when he was four years old. Mozart wrote a lot of music for the piano.

Stevie Wonder is a famous keyboard player. Although he is blind, he learnt to play the piano when he was very young. He also sings and writes songs.

New music

People play electronic keyboards in **jazz**, **rock** and **pop** music today. Many keyboards have a drum **rhythm**. Keyboards can be linked to computers to play many new sounds.

You can also hear the **synthesizer** in rock and pop music. Synthesizers play many different sounds. Jean-Michel Jarre uses synthesizers and laser lights in his open-air concerts.

Sound activity

You can make up your own music on the piano. Make up some music that sounds like rain falling. Make it slow and gentle. Then make it faster and louder.

Ask a grown-up to lift the lid of a piano. Then ask them to play some notes. Stand on a chair and look inside the piano. Can you see the hammers hit the strings?

Thinking about keyboards

You can find the answers to all of these questions in this book.

1. Why are the instruments in this book called keyboard instruments?

2. What is a piano duet?

3. How do you play the accordion?

4. What is a harmonium?

Glossary

accompany to go with

amplifier something that changes electrical signals into sounds by sending them through a loud speaker
You say ampli-fire

bellows pump used to direct air into the soundpipes of an instrument

composer person who writes new music

jazz old style of music from America that is often made up as it is played

musical a musical is a play set to music, with songs and dancing

orchestra large group of musicians who play their musical instruments together
You say ork-es-tra

plucks pulls

pop music music of the last fifty years. A lot of people like this music.

reed thin strip of cane or metal

rhythm repeated beats or sounds that make a pattern
You say rith-um

rock music kind of pop music with a strong beat

synthesizer electronic instrument that can make or change many different sounds
You say sintha-size-a

trio music for three players or a group of three musicians
You say tree-o

upright piano piano in which the strings stand up against the soundboard

vibrate move up and down or from side to side very quickly

31

Index

HFL version

Titles in the *Musical Instuments* series include:

Hardback   0 431 12900 2

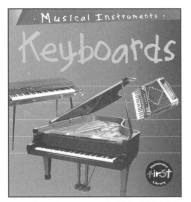

Hardback   0 431 12904 5

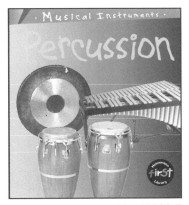

Hardback   0 431 12903 7

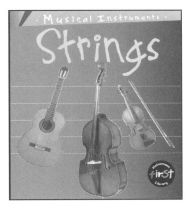

Hardback   0 431 12902 9

Hardback   0 431 12901 0

Find out about the other titles in this series on our website www.heinemann.co.uk/library